echo
BOOKS

An imprint of
Wintertickle PRESS

Acknowledgement: A special thank you goes out to all the teachers and consultants who contributed to this project with their suggestions, proofreading and invaluable input.

Various photo and writing credits can be found throughout the book. Stock photos are credited to iStockphoto or Dreamstime. For queries or more information, please contact the publisher directly.

Disclaimer: Wintertickle Press endeavours to have up-to-date information regarding the Ontario Secondary School Literacy Test (OSSLT) at the time of publication. However, this information changes often. For details on the specifics of the OSSLT, please check with the Educational Quality and Accountability Office (EQAO) website at www.eqao.com. Wintertickle Press made every reasonable effort to check the accuracy of website addresses at the time of publication, however due to the transient nature of the Internet, cannot warrant their accuracy. Wintertickle Press does not warrant the information about the OSSLT in this book to be accurate. This publication is for literacy educational purposes only and does not guarantee a student will pass the OSSLT.

Published and distributed by:

Wintertickle **PRESS**

132 Commerce Park Drive, Unit K, Suite 155
Barrie, ON, L4N 0Z7

echo
BOOKS

WintericklePress.com

Printed and bound in Canada

ISBN 978-1-894813-71-6

Table of Contents

Introduction: what this book is all about

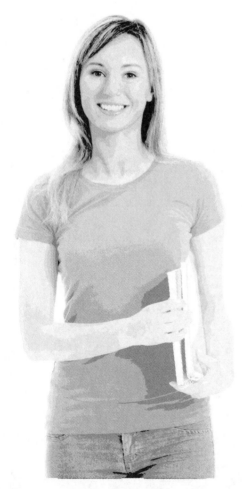

Hello there! Welcome to the *OSSLT Literacy Lab*. My name is Paige and I am from North Bay. This student workbook has various practice activities or labs for each aspect of the Ontario Secondary School Literacy Test or the OSSLT for short. The book is divided into three sections: a section with reading practice, a section with writing practice and a section with a practice test. You can use this book to work on the skills you need a little extra practice with, or you can work through the entire book cover to cover. I hope this helps you prepare for the OSSLT and gives you some tools to help you achieve your potential.

SECTION 1

Section 1: The OSSLT Reading Lab

The OSSLT uses different selections of reading materials to measure your literacy skills. There are five specific types of reading selections you will encounter on the test: information paragraph, news report, dialogue, real-life narrative and graphic text.

Using these texts, you will be asked to answer both multiple-choice and open-response questions.

The questions are designed to measure three different types of reading skills. The first skill is to find information to answer questions directly in the text itself. Sometimes the answer will be in one sentence, or it may be in several locations.

The second reading skill deals with indirectly stated ideas and information. To find the answers for these questions, you will need to use facts, details and information from the reading selection as clues in order to make reasonable assumptions about what is not directly found in the text.

The third reading skill is demonstrated when you are able to make connections between the information in the reading selection and your personal knowledge and experience. The answer for these questions comes from your own experiences, beliefs and background. You have to think beyond the reading selection to answer these types of questions.

More information on the reading skills required for the OSSLT can be found on the EQAO website at www.eqao.com.

In this resource, you will be walked through two examples of each type of reading activity similar to those you will encounter on the OSSLT. You will find advice from fictional representations of typical Ontario students. Tips will be provided in the form of notes that are "paper-clipped" to your activities for ease of reference.

Tip: Be sure to try the great suggestions in these notes throughout the selections.

You will know you have not completed all the questions for a particular reading selection and will have to turn the page to continue if you see an arrow that says "Turn the page to complete this section."

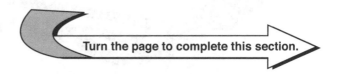

Turn the page to complete this section.

You will know you have completed a section when you see the phrase "End of Section" in a grey rectangular box.

End of Section.

Information Paragraph: conveys information on a particular topic

. . . .

Hi. My name is Marcus and I am from Nepean. The most difficult thing for me with information paragraphs is finding the main idea. A main idea deals with the point, thought or opinion being expressed in a paragraph. Here's a tip that really helped me locate and understand the main idea of a paragraph. Give it a try. I always ask questions such as: What is this paragraph trying to say? What is it about? and What is the point being made? Then I reread the paragraph, looking for answers. This helps me figure out what the main point is. When I am done reading, I try to connect the information to things I already know. If I still have questions, I read the paragraph again.

Read the selection below and answer the following questions.

Tip: The numbers at the side of the selection indicate line numbers.

0 Provincial Park is an example of one location existing for a variety of purposes.
Established in 1893, it is the oldest provincial park in Canada. It is approximately 7,653
square kilometres. In size, this is about one and a half times the size of the province of
Prince Edward Island. Because of its vast size and proximity to major populated areas
such as Ottawa and Toronto, Algonquin is one of the most popular provincial parks   5
in Canada. Algonquin Park is located between Georgian Bay and the Ottawa River in
Central Ontario, and an east–west road, Highway 60, runs right through the south end
of the park. Besides having over 2,400 lakes and 1,200 kilometres of streams and rivers,
Algonquin Provincial Park also has visitor interpretation programs, historic structures,
camps, administration buildings and museums. The park offers many different seasonal   10
activities such as day hiking, camping, canoeing, mountain biking, horseback riding and
cross-country skiing. Interestingly, Algonquin is the only designated park in Ontario to
allow industrial logging to take place. Those managing Algonquin Provincial Park work
hard to balance tourism, conservation, research and industry so its many purposes can
exist in harmony all in one location. Although Algonquin Park has been around for a   15
long time, it is a gem that provides enjoyment for its many yearly visitors.

Tip: While reading, think about Algonquin Park and ask yourself questions about it.

Multiple-Choice (Circle the best or most correct answer.)

1 How large is Algonquin Provincial Park?

    A half the size of Prince Edward Island

    B one and a half times the size of Prince Edward Island

    C twice the size of Prince Edward Island

    D half the size of Quebec City

2 Why is Algonquin Provincial Park popular with tourists?

    A It is extremely far from urban centres.

    B It has museums.

    C There are a lot of activities.

    D It is a small park.

3 Which line demonstrates the use of commas to separate items in a list?

    A line 2

    B line 8

    C line 11

    D line 15

4 Which of the following is closest in meaning to the word "gem" as used in line 16?

    A something special

    B precious stone

    C location with lots of rocks

    D jewellery

5 What is the purpose of this selection?

    A to let readers know there is a lot to do at Algonquin Provincial Park

    B to provide facts on the size of the park

    C to describe the exact location of Algonquin Provincial Park

    D to explain that Algonquin Provincial Park serves many purposes

Tip: Go back and read the word "gem" in context in the paragraph. The best answer is not the literal meaning of "gem."

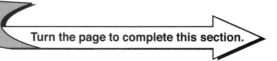

Turn the page to complete this section.

Reading: Information Paragraph

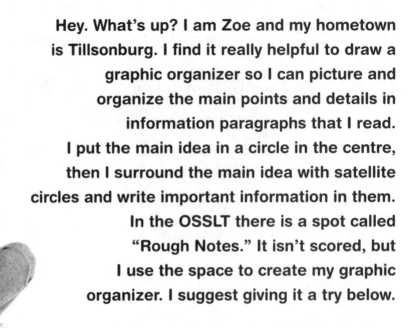

Hey. What's up? I am Zoe and my hometown is Tillsonburg. I find it really helpful to draw a graphic organizer so I can picture and organize the main points and details in information paragraphs that I read. I put the main idea in a circle in the centre, then I surround the main idea with satellite circles and write important information in them. In the OSSLT there is a spot called "Rough Notes." It isn't scored, but I use the space to create my graphic organizer. I suggest giving it a try below.

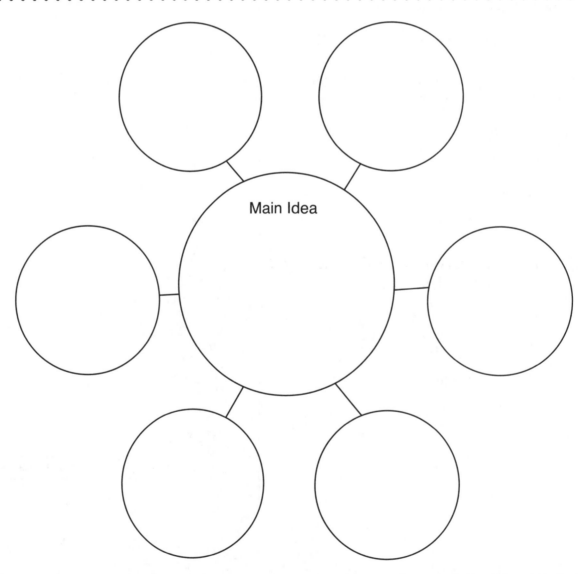

Main Idea

6 State a main idea of this selection, and provide one specific detail from the selection that supports it.

_____

_____

_____

_____

_____

_____

Tip: Remember the main idea is the point, thought or opinion being expressed in an information paragraph.

7 Do you think Algonquin Provincial Park would be an interesting place to visit? Use information from the selection to support your answer.

_____

_____

_____

_____

_____

_____

Tip: Here is a chance to draw upon your own experiences and use information from the paragraph.

Rough Notes
This space below is for rough notes. Nothing you write in this area will be marked.

Tip: When you see "End of Section" you know you have come to the end of the questions for a particular activity.

End of Section.

Reading: Information Paragraph

Hi there. I'm Carter and I live in Kenora. What I find challenging about information paragraphs is figuring out how they are organized. I look for transition words or connectors to give me clues. These words and phrases improve logical organization and make a paragraph easier to understand. They also help me to see links between thoughts. I look for connecting words and phrases when I read information paragraphs. Some common ways a paragraph can be organized are chronological order, general to specific, cause and effect, and compare and contrast.

This chart provides examples of common ways paragraphs are organized and the connecting words and phrases often associated with them.

Organization Type	Common Connectors
Chronological order	first, next, then, initially, before, after, when, finally, preceding, following
General to specific	for instance, for example, such as, to illustrate, a colon (:) followed by a list
Cause and effect	as a result of, because of, in order to, may be due to, effects of, therefore, consequently, for this reason, if, thus
Compare and contrast	as well as, different from, same as, similar to, as opposed to, instead of, although, however, compared with, either/or

Read the selection below and answer the following questions.

Ontario Northland Railway operates a Canadian passenger train called the Polar
Bear Express, which is the lifeline connecting Cochrane and Moosonee. Initially,
this rail service was introduced back in 1964. There aren't any roads to Moosonee, so
supplies and people often come in and out by train. Although the official designation
for the Polar Bear Express is "passenger train," it also carries cargo such as canoes,   5
snowmobiles, all-terrain vehicles, cars and light trucks. The Polar Bear Express
currently operates five days per week year-round, and during the summer there are
additional trains added to the schedule. Before 2012, this train had a full dining car in
the summer months, but that has been discontinued. This Canadian passenger train
is not to be confused with the children's book by Chris Van Allsburg similarly named   10
The Polar Express. This vital service connecting these communities continues to be an
important part of Ontario's north.

Tip: Circle
any important
facts to help
you understand
more about
the Polar Bear
Express.

Photo Credits: Kim Forster. Used with permission.

Multiple-Choice (Circle the best or most correct answer.)

1 Why is the Polar Bear Express considered a lifeline to the people of Moosonee?

    A There are no roads leading to Moosonee.

    B It has a dining car providing food for the residents of Moosonee.

    C It is a passenger train.

    D It carries trucks to Moosonee.

2 Which word is closest in meaning to "vital" as used in line 11?

    A optional

    B expendable

    C necessary

    D useful

3 Why is "*The Polar Express*" italicized at the end of the paragraph?

    A to give emphasis

    B to indicate that it is a title of a book

    C to show that it is a train

    D to indicate that it is the end of the paragraph

4 Why would the train run more often in the summer?

    A People eat more in the summer.

    B The weather is better.

    C There is a greater need for supplies in the summer.

    D There is more tourism in the summer.

5 How are lines 5–6 grouped?

    A by the schedule

    B by what the train carries

    C by who uses the train

    D by the reasons the train exists

Tip: Read all four answers before choosing one. You are looking for the best possible answer.

6 State a main idea of this selection, and provide one specific detail from the selection that supports it.

Tip: The number of lines gives you an indication of how much you should write.

_____

_____

_____

_____

_____

_____

Rough Notes
This space below is for rough notes. Nothing you write in this area will be marked.

Tip: This is the perfect place to create a graphic organizer.

End of Section.

News Report: a news story that presents information in a particular format that answers the questions Who? What? Where? When? Why? and How?

. . . .

Hello. My name is Sitarah and I am from Brampton. I often read news reports online. They answer the questions Who? What? Where? When? Why? and How? I often had difficulties answering questions after reading a news report until my brother gave me a tip that I've used ever since. He told me to read the questions quickly before reading the report. That way, I know what to look for when reading the selection. My brother's advice usually isn't that good, and I often don't pay attention to a lot of the things he says. However, I found this tip really helpful and I now do this for all the reading activities. Try it and see if it helps you too.

Read the selection below and answer the following questions.

Reality Prank Show Turns the Tables on Students

A high school wrestling team changed its name—and mascot—from Huskies to Unicorns. This is one of the pranks played on teens from around Greater Toronto in a new, Canadian reality show which premiered Tuesday night. 1

The pranks were conducted at 20 schools—in Brampton, Mississauga and Richmond Hill, to name a few—set up by host Lisa Gilroy with the help, and approval, of principals and teachers. 2

While some may question the ethics of playing jokes on kids at school, the show's producer says it was deliberately harmless and all in good fun. No one teen was singled out—entire classes were involved—and everyone from principal to parent signed off on the prank before it was approved to go on air. "We basically wanted to do a prank show that had never been done before, with teachers and principals getting the kids," said Mitch Burman, supervising producer and director. 3

"It's a kind of double-cross; it's usually the kids who are being the pranksters in class. We let the teachers and principals get a little payback." 4

The Peel District School Board agreed to be part of the show and a Bolton high school—Humberview—was involved in transforming its wrestlers into unicorns. 5

Carla Pereira, manager of communications for the Peel District School Board said, "The principal made it very clear that the prank needed to be pre-approved. It was reviewed by the principal and other staff, and they were also consulted on which team would be pranked." 6

She said the "production team was very co-operative and focused on making it a positive experience for students. My understanding, from the principal, is that the students loved the experience." 7

The show was created by a Canadian television production company. Pereira said parents were initially made aware that their children "would be videotaped for a 'commercial'—that was the prank. Students and parents signed consent afterwards to permit the footage to be aired." 8

Adapted from the article "Reality prank show Undercover High turns the tables on Toronto students" by Kristin Rushowy, published in *Toronto Star*, June 17, 2014. Licensed from *Toronto Star* for republication in *The OSSLT Literacy Lab*—Torstar Syndication Services.

Multiple-Choice (Circle the best or most correct answer.)

1 Why did the wrestling team change its name from Huskies to Unicorns?

    A They changed schools.

    B They liked the new name better.

    C Their coach insisted they change it.

    D They were being pranked for a reality show.

2 Why were entire classes pranked instead of individual students?

    A to prevent singling anyone out

    B to make filming easier

    C to involve more people

    D to please the producer

3 According to the supervising producer, what did teachers enjoy most about being part of this project?

    A being tricky

    B punishing students

    C showing students they could be fun

    D being on TV

4 Which word is closest in meaning to "ethics" as used in paragraph 3?

    A committees

    B morals

    C reasons

    D decisions

Tip: If you don't understand a word, read the sentence before and after it, looking for clues.

5 How is paragraph 1 organized?

    A specific details to general information

    B general information to specific details

    C chronological order

    D comparing and contrasting

Tip: After reading the answers, eliminate any that are incorrect.

Hey there. My name is Chun and I am from Markham. To really understand a news article, I answer the questions Who? What? Where? When? Why? and How? I simply say the answers aloud then write them in boxes. I find this really helps me understand the article and gives me a great visual to see what the news report was all about. It's easy to do. Try it below.

Who?
_____
_____

What?
_____
_____

Where?
_____
_____

When?
_____
_____

Why?
_____
_____

How?
_____
_____

6 Why did students and staff find it a positive experience to be on a reality prank TV show? Use specific details from the selection to support your answer.

Tip: Support your answer with relevant details from the news report.

_____

_____

_____

_____

_____

_____

Rough Notes

This space below is for rough notes. Nothing you write in this area will be marked.

End of Section.

Read the selection below and answer the following questions.

Hitchhiking Robot to Journey Across Canada

With pool noodle arms, a plastic bucket for a torso and a limitless wealth of retrievable knowledge—at least while in the 3G network range—a curious entity is getting ready to put out the thumb and hitch rides across Canada this summer. It's HitchBOT, the genderless hitchhiking robot that will rely on the kindness of flesh-and-blood strangers to safely complete a 4,480-kilometre odyssey that starts in Halifax on July 27 and is supposed to wind up at an art gallery in Victoria. 1

At least that's the hope. Like every cross-continental ramble, this one's a gamble. "There's this idea of adventure, exploration, optimism," said David Harris Smith, a McMaster University researcher who's spearheading the "social robotics" experiment with Ryerson's Frauke Zeller, an assistant professor in communications. 2

"It kind of depends upon empathy and social collaboration," Harris Smith added. "That's one of the risks we're willing to take." 3

Conceived through discussions that began last year, the HitchBOT project involves students and professors. The team is using speech-recognition software so that HitchBOT can converse with the people it meets, as well as network connectivity to allow it to search 4 for regionally-relevant talking points and post photos and text to social media.

The robot will be about the size of a six-year-old child that will include a built-in car seat that can be buckled up next to a driver. 5

The plan is to simply leave HitchBOT on the side of the road in Halifax. When someone comes to pick it up, the robot will tell them where it's headed, and ask them how far they're going. 6

Harris Smith said the robot's conversation software will allow it to "negotiate" the details of its ride and request to be plugged in so that it can recharge its battery. At the end of the ride, HitchBOT will ask to be left safely on the side of the road, where it will wait with its thumb out to be picked up again. 7

Photo courtesy of HitchBOT / hitchBOT.me. Used with permission.

Adapted from the article "Hitchhiking robot to journey across Canada this summer" by Alex Ballingall, published in *Toronto Star*, June 17, 2014. Licensed from *Toronto Star* for republication in *The OSSLT Literacy Lab*—Torstar Syndication Services.

Multiple-Choice (Circle the best or most correct answer.)

1 According to the selection, what did David Harris Smith hope HitchBOT would accomplish?

    A create awareness about car seat safety

    B communicate with various people across Canada

    C hitchhike across Canada and rely on the kindness of strangers

    D gather information from across Canada

2 What type of details will HitchBOT "negotiate" when it is picked up for a ride?

    A where it is headed and how to recharge its battery

    B regionally-relevant talking points

    C posting photos and texts to social media

    D the length of its trip

3 What is this "social robotics" experiment really about?

    A robotic speech

    B adventure and travel

    C demonstrating the advances in robotics

    D empathy and co-operation

4 Which word is closest in meaning to "odyssey" as used in paragraph 1?

    A occurrence

    B experiment

    C journey

    D strange

5 Which event described in the selection happened first?

    A Students and professors discussed the idea of HitchBOT.

    B HitchBOT was built with pool noodle arms and a plastic bucket for a torso.

    C Speech-recognition software was installed in HitchBOT.

    D HitchBOT was dropped at the side of the road in Halifax.

Tip: Don't leave a question blank. Make an educated guess as a last resort.

6 Why did David Harris Smith and Frauke Zeller conduct this experiment? Use specific details from the selection to support your answer.

Tip: Remember to check your response for errors.

_____

_____

_____

_____

_____

_____

Rough Notes

This space below is for rough notes. Nothing you write in this area will be marked.

End of Section.

Dialogue: a conversation that occurs between two or more people

Hey. My name is Charlotte and I am from Barrie. Sometimes reading a dialogue will mess me up. So now I do two things. The first thing I do is pretend that I am reading a movie script, and I visualize or play the conversation in my head as if it were a film. I even imagine details like what the people in the dialogue look like. This helps to give meaning to the conversation for me. The second thing I do is pay attention to who is talking in the dialogue. I do this by noticing words that give me a clue that it might be a new speaker including words like "said," "paused," "exclaimed," "replied," etc. I also take note of when it is a new paragraph. Often times this indicates a change in who is speaking in the dialogue.

Read the selection below and answer the following questions.

Tip: The numbers at the side indicate the paragraph number.

Sofie took a deep breath and knocked on Mr. Patel's office door. 1

"Come in," called Mr. Patel. "What can I do for you?" 2

"Well," Sofie hesitated. She was nervous talking to adults. "I have an idea for fundraising for the school library." 3

"Oh." Mr. Patel raised his eyebrows. "This sounds interesting. I would like to hear what you have to say. Please share your idea, Sofie." 4

"Well, lots of people have books at home that they've read and don't need anymore. What about organizing a book drive, then having a sale in the library? It would be a type of used-book fair." 5

Mr. Patel paused. "But who will sell the books, and how will we get people to attend it?" 6

"I know lots of students who would love to help, and my dad is good friends with a famous author. I'm sure we could get him to come in and speak." 7

"And advertising…?" 8

"We could post it on the school's website and put it in the newsletters. There is also the sign in front of the school. We could include information during morning announcements and put posters up." 9

"Sounds like you've thought this through, Sofie. I think it just might work," Mr. Patel remarked, rather impressed. 10

"Thank you, Mr. Patel." 11

Sofie thought to herself, "I didn't need to be nervous at all!" 12

Tip: Each new paragraph represents a change of speaker in this selection.

Multiple-Choice (Circle the best or most correct answer.)

1 Why did Sofie take a deep breath before knocking on Mr. Patel's office door?

    A She was tired.

    B She was nervous.

    C She was confident.

    D She did not like Mr. Patel.

2 Why did Sofie want to talk to Mr. Patel?

    A She had a fundraising idea.

    B She loved books.

    C She wanted better grades.

    D She wanted to bring a famous author to the school.

3 Which word is closest in meaning to "impressed" (paragraph 10)?

    A imprinted

    B imitated

    C bored

    D pleased

4 What does "it" refer to in paragraph 6?

    A advertising

    B book drive

    C used-book fair

    D newsletter

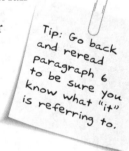

Tip: Go back and reread Paragraph 6 to be sure you know what "it" is referring to.

5 According to the selection, what would be most persuasive to Mr. Patel about his decision to support a used-book fair?

    A the money that could be made

    B the details had been thought through

    C the advertising

    D the books

6 Identify why you think Sofie was nervous to see Mr. Patel. Use specific details from the selection to support your answer.

Tip: Go back to the reading selection to find specific details to use in your response.

_____

_____

_____

_____

_____

_____

7 Identify examples of how Sofie had thoroughly thought through the details of a used-book fair. Use specific details from the selection to support your answer.

_____

_____

_____

_____

_____

_____

Rough Notes

This space below is for rough notes. Nothing you write in this area will be marked.

End of Section.

Read the selection below and answer the following questions.

Connor packed his suitcase and sighed as he squeezed it shut. He didn't particularly want to work at a camp as a counsellor-in-training this summer, but his parents had insisted he do something "productive" with his time off. **1**

"Are you ready to go?" Connor's dad called up the stairs. **2**

"Almost," Connor quipped back. He picked up his suitcase in one hand and grabbed his phone in the other. He just received a text and was curious who it might be. **3**

"I'm coming," Connor said as he made his way down the stairs. **4**

"Great. Let's put that suitcase in the car and get going before heavy traffic sets in." **5**

Connor started to read his text. It was from his good friend, Raj. **6**

"Who's that from?" Connor's dad queried as he started the car engine. **7**

"Raj." **8**

"Oh, that's nice. He's probably wishing you luck as a counsellor-in-training. You know, Connor, I completely understand that you aren't too excited about leaving your friends and going up north. But this will be such a terrific experience. You will meet new people, take on responsibility and get volunteer hours too. The lake at the camp is fabulous. I really think you are going to warm to the idea as time goes on." **9**

"Yes, I think you are right, Dad," Connor answered. **10**

Connor's dad was surprised by the change in tone in his son's voice. "Well, you sound a lot more chipper," he exclaimed. **11**

"I am." Connor smiled mischievously. "You know that was Raj who texted me, right?" **12**

"Yes." **13**

Connor was laughing, "His parents have signed him up to be a counsellor-in-training at the same camp." **14**

His father smiled, "Well, what do you know? That's good news for Raj, you and me." **15**

Multiple-Choice (Circle the best or most correct answer.)

1 What is the purpose of this reading selection?

    A to compare summer camps

    B to describe driving

    C to entertain with an anecdote

    D to explain counsellor-in-training

2 What had Connor's parents insisted he do this summer?

    A get a job

    B go to camp

    C spend time with Raj

    D be productive

3 Which is closest in meaning to "queried" as used in paragraph 7?

    A asked

    B answered

    C yelled

    D said

Tip: Go back and reread the sentence in the selection replacing "queried" with each option.

4 Which of the following is **not** a reason Connor's father listed for working as a counsellor-in-training?

    A to meet new people

    B to get away from friends

    C to take on responsibility

    D to get volunteer hours

5 Why did Connor sound a lot happier after getting the text from Raj?

    A Connor no longer had to go to camp.

    B Raj was going to visit Connor.

    C Raj was going to be a counsellor-in-training at the same camp.

    D Raj was coming over to say goodbye.

Turn the page to complete this section.

6 Why did Connor's father want Connor to be a counsellor-in-training? Use specific details from the selection to support your answer.

_____

_____

_____

_____

_____

_____

7 Why was Raj's text good news for Raj, Connor and Connor's father? Use specific details from the selection to support your answer.

_____

_____

_____

_____

_____

_____

Rough Notes
This space below is for rough notes. Nothing you write in this area will be marked.

End of Section.

Real-Life Narrative: an account of an important time or event in someone's life

. . . .

Hello there. My name is Aiden and I am from Toronto. I really enjoy reading real-life narratives—especially if they are about a person I am interested in. To make sure I understand a narrative, I quickly read the selection first to get an idea of what it is about. Then, when I read the entire narrative more carefully, I try to look for links between what I am reading and the experiences I have had in my own life. Sometimes the experiences I am reading about are so similar to some I have had, I just feel like I am in the story. Sometimes they are quite different. In those cases, I try to imagine being in the story. This helps me understand it better.

Read the selection below and answer the following questions.

Adam Beach is a Role Model

Photo courtesy of the Canadian Film Centre/Phillip Chin

1 After a long list of over 60 film and TV roles, actor Adam Beach was excited to return to Canada to star in the TV series *Arctic Air*, which ran from 2012–2014. Adam played the character of Bobby Martin. This starring role gave Adam mainstream notoriety here at home in Canada.

2 Adam, a member of the Ojibwa Nation, has worked alongside many actors in both Canada and the United States, including the likes of Harrison Ford and Daniel Craig.

3 Adam was born in Ashern, Manitoba, and when he was young, he and his two brothers lived on the Lake Manitoba Dog Creek First Nation Reserve. Adam's rise to fame wasn't without challenges, however—when Adam was only eight years old, his parents died only months apart. Adam and his brother went to live with his grandmother until he was 12. Then the boys were taken to Winnipeg where they stayed with an aunt and uncle.

4 While in high school, Adam discovered drama. He began performing in local theatre productions and took a lead role at the Manitoba Theatre for Young People.

5 In recent years, Adam has started several charity initiatives and believes in giving back to his community. There is a special spot in his heart for youth and film, and he supports both. He is involved with the National Aboriginal Achievement Foundation. He also travels to schools, conferences and other events to speak candidly about the challenges he has faced in his life and his road to success.

Of his role on *Arctic Air*, Adam talks about his connection to Bobby, the character he plays: "I do a lot of inspirational talks for kids, to motivate them to change their lives and give them hope. And I found that this character shares a lot of those qualities. A lot of the communities I connect to get their inspiration from television and YouTube. I felt that this character could reach out to them and really connect. He's a character who's struggling with himself. He's trying to get back in touch with the person he once was." 6

Beyond playing roles on TV, Adam has proved he is also a role model, spreading hope and also encouragement. Although acting in *Arctic Air* has been a major part of his career, who knows what's next for Adam Beach? 7

Tip: Look for root words inside larger words that you don't understand.

© Feature flash | Dreamstime.com - Adam Beach Photo

Multiple-Choice (Circle the best or most correct answer.)

1 Which of the following is Adam Beach's birthplace?

    A Winnipeg

    B Ojibwa

    C Ashbern

    D Dog Creek

2 At what point did Adam first become interested in acting?

    A when he was in high school

    B when he went to live with his grandmother

    C when he was chosen to act in *Arctic Air*

    D when he acted with Harrison Ford and Daniel Craig

3 Which word is closest in meaning to "notoriety" as used in paragraph 1?

    A disrepute

    B fame

    C influence

    D publicity

4 What are two focuses of Adam's charities?

    A television and film

    B high school and community

    C drama and film

    D youth and film

5 Why are commas used in paragraph 2?

    A They link two independent clauses.

    B They separate items in a series.

    C They set off added information.

    D They set off introductory elements.

6 What best describes paragraph 6?

    A a direct quote

    B an indirect quote

    C an illustration

    D a description

7 According to the selection, what is the most likely reason Adam feels the need to share his story as an inspirational speaker?

    A to gain notoriety

    B to promote and encourage people to watch television

    C to encourage children who are facing challenges

    D to promote *Arctic Air*

8 Why is paragraph 7 an effective conclusion?

    A It provides unusual information about Adam.

    B The question suggests that Adam will have future accomplishments.

    C It adds additional information.

    D It introduces a new idea.

Tip: If you don't know a particular answer, reread relevant parts of the narrative.

End of Section.

Read the selection below and answer the following questions.

Eileen Vollick

Photo Credit: Canada Aviation and Space Museum

On March 13, 1928, 19-year-old Eileen Vollick took the day off work in order to take her federal aviation test. The textile analyst, who worked for the Hamilton Cotton Company, successfully passed the flight test to become the first woman in Canada to qualify as a pilot as well as the first woman in the world to be trained on a ski plane.

1

Although this event granted Eileen a sort of "celebrity-status," it was not always an easy path for this Wiarton-born textile analyst and assistant designer. Eileen had watched pilots take off and land at Jack V. Elliot's Air Service and wanted the opportunity to fly herself.

2

Eileen applied for flight training, but because she was a woman, Jack Elliot wouldn't accept her as a student until the Department of National Defence gave their approval. The Department took three months to approve her application and insisted she be 19 years old even though the age requirement for men was 17. While waiting to turn 19, Eileen became the first Canadian woman to parachute out on the wings of a Curtiss JN-4 plane and parachuted into Hamilton Bay, which is now known as Burlington Bay.

3

The first flight instructor assigned to her didn't want a female student so—even though it was against the rules—he did spins, loops, and zooms on the first lesson. He was attempting to frighten Eileen, but it didn't work.

4

However, Eileen's next two instructors welcomed her. She also felt accepted by her 35 classmates who were all male students. Eileen had to take her lessons at 6 a.m.

5

throughout the winter so she could get to work by 8:30 a.m. Determination and hard work were small sacrifices to reach her goal.

It took courage and determination for women to be fully accepted in the new flying movement. Some women weren't allowed to sign up for lessons, and others were subjected to a more rigorous set of rules, or they faced instructors who tried to scare them off. However, women in aviation grew in numbers and impact thanks in no small part to Eileen Vollick for bravely becoming Canada's first female pilot.

6

Photo Credit: Canada Aviation and Space Museum

Tip: To improve understanding, try putting long sentences into your own words.

Multiple-Choice (Circle the best or most correct answer.)

1 Why did Eileen want to become a pilot?

    A She had watched pilots take off and land at an airport.

    B She wanted to become the first female pilot in Canada.

    C She wanted to help Canada's efforts in the war.

    D She enjoyed taking on a challenge.

2 What was **not** one of Eileen's accomplishments?

    A first woman to be trained on a ski plane

    B first woman to fly solo

    C first woman to parachute from a Curtiss JN-4 plane

    D first Canadian woman to qualify as a pilot

3 Which word is closest in meaning to "rigorous" as used in paragraph 6?

    A careful

    B accurate

    C attentive

    D demanding

4 What was one thing that Eileen did that demonstrated her determination?

    A She quit her regular job as a textile analyst.

    B She listened to critical comments from male students.

    C She took her lessons early in the morning before she went to work.

    D She broke rules while flying.

5 Why are two dashes used in paragraph 4?

    A to emphasize the content between the dashes

    B to clarify a list in the sentence

    C to add descriptiveness to the sentence

    D to join words in the sentence

6 Why did Jack Elliot finally allow Eileen to take flight training?

    A She received approval from the Department of Defence.

    B She turned 17 years old.

    C She had already parachuted from a Curtiss JN-4.

    D She had already performed spins, loops and zooms.

7 What is the purpose of paragraphs 3, 4 and 5?

    A to show the ways different people supported Eileen

    B to describe the typical life of a pilot

    C to describe the challenges Eileen faced

    D to add humour to the story

End of Section.

Graphic Text: illustrates information with the assistance of graphic features, such as pictures, diagrams, drawings, schedules, maps, charts or tables

· ·

Hi. I'm Jia and I am from Harrow. When I look at graphic text, it usually has captions to give me an overview of what it is all about. After reading the captions, I enjoy seeing if I can get a solid idea about the selection by looking at the graphics. To confirm my interpretation of the "picture" part of the material, I then carefully read all the text associated with the article. Graphic text is a really good way to display a lot of information with few words.

Read the selection below and answer the following questions.

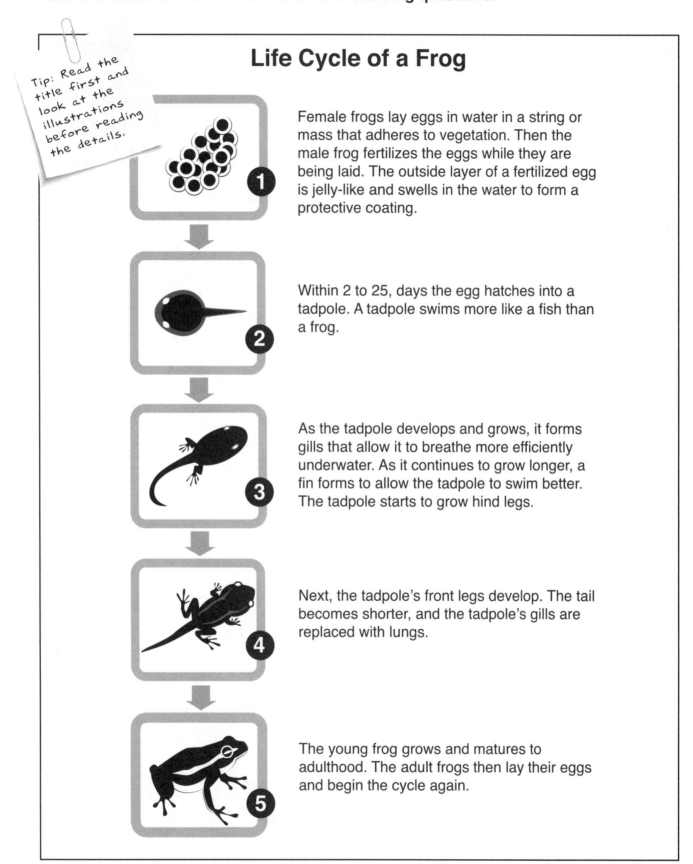

Life Cycle of a Frog

Tip: Read the title first and look at the illustrations before reading the details.

1 Female frogs lay eggs in water in a string or mass that adheres to vegetation. Then the male frog fertilizes the eggs while they are being laid. The outside layer of a fertilized egg is jelly-like and swells in the water to form a protective coating.

2 Within 2 to 25, days the egg hatches into a tadpole. A tadpole swims more like a fish than a frog.

3 As the tadpole develops and grows, it forms gills that allow it to breathe more efficiently underwater. As it continues to grow longer, a fin forms to allow the tadpole to swim better. The tadpole starts to grow hind legs.

4 Next, the tadpole's front legs develop. The tail becomes shorter, and the tadpole's gills are replaced with lungs.

5 The young frog grows and matures to adulthood. The adult frogs then lay their eggs and begin the cycle again.

Multiple-Choice (Circle the best or most correct answer.)

1 According to the selection, where do frogs most often lay their eggs?

    A on the shore

    B in the trees

    C in the water

    D in the sand

2 Which word is closest in meaning to "develops" as used in Stage 3?

    A declines

    B slows

    C matures

    D diminishes

3 Which feature in this graphic text best identifies chronological order?

    A title

    B numbers

    C pictures

    D text

4 Which stage could be considered both the beginning and the end of the life cycle of a frog?

    A Stage 1

    B Stage 2

    C Stage 4

    D Stage 5

5 When does a tadpole become a better swimmer?

    A when it forms a fin

    B when it forms gills

    C when it forms front legs

    D when it forms hind legs

Tip: Rephrase question 5 as a statement using each answer in the sentence to see which is correct.

End of Section.

Read the selection below and answer the following questions.

South City Community Pool Schedule
Hours of operation: weekdays: 10:00 a.m.–6:00 p.m.   weekends: 10:00 a.m.–4:00 p.m.

Time	Mon	Tues	Wed	Thus	Fri	Sat	Sun
10:00 a.m.	adult laps	aqua fit	laps	aqua fit	adult laps	laps	aqua fit
11:00 a.m.	parent & tots	school groups	parents & tots	school groups	aqua fit	family swim	lessons
12:00 noon	aqua fit	parent & tots	school groups	parents & tots	school groups	family swim	family swim
1:00 p.m.	lessons	aqua fit	lessons	lessons	school groups	lessons	family swim
2:00 p.m.	diving club	swim team practice	diving club	school groups	diving club	lessons	family swim
3:00 p.m.	free swim	lessons	free swim	lessons	free swim	lessons	family swim
4:00 p.m.	lessons	laps	laps	free swim	lessons	closed	closed
5:00 p.m.	laps	free swim	lessons	laps	swim team practice	closed	closed

Descriptions:

Adult laps: The pool is divided into lanes and is open for lap swimming for adults over the age of 18.

*Aqua fit: Aqua fit offers exercise classes in the pool. Check front desk for more information and registration. There is an extra fee for aqua fit.

Diving club: The South City Community Diving Club uses the pool at this time.

Family swim: This is a time for parents and children to enjoy the pool. The slide is open at this time.

Free swim: Open for all to come and enjoy the pool. The slide is open at this time.

Laps: The pool is divided into lanes and is open for swimming.

*Lessons: The South City Community Pool offers lessons to swimmers of all ages and skill levels. Check with the front desk for more information and registration. There is an extra fee for lessons.

Parents & tots: The pool is open for parents and their children under the age of four. All children must be accompanied by an adult.

School groups: This time is available to various local schools to book in advance.

Swim team practice. The South City Community Swim Team has designated practice time.

*Registration is required for these activities. An additional fee will apply.

Multiple-Choice (Circle the best or most correct answer.)

1 Which activities require registration and an extra fee?

    A parents & tots

    B free swim and laps

    C school groups and adult laps

    D aqua fit and lessons

2 How is the schedule organized?

    A by comparing and contrasting

    B by chronological order

    C by cause and effect

    D in order of importance

3 According to the schedule, when can a 12-year-old child go to the pool to swim laps?

    A Monday, 10:00 a.m.

    B Tuesday, 4:00 p.m.

    C Friday, 11:00 p.m.

    D Saturday, 2:00 p.m.

4 Which feature of this graphic text identifies the schedule?

    A arrows

    B description

    C table

    D lessons

5 According to the schedule, if you wanted to use the recreational slide, when would be the best time to go to South City Community Pool?

    A Sunday, 12:00 noon

    B Tuesday, 4:00 p.m.

    C Monday, 12:00 noon

    D Wednesday, 5:00 p.m.

6 Why are there asterisks (*) beside "aqua fit" and "lessons" in the description?

    A to indicate to the reader that there is more information about those activities

    B to highlight those activities

    C to show the reader how the material is organized

    D to improve the appearance of the schedule

Tip: Go back to the selection to find all the places where asterisks (*) occur.

End of Section.

SECTION 2

Section 2: The OSSLT Writing Lab

The OSSLT assesses your writing skills through several different tasks. You will be expected to complete long-writing tasks, short-writing tasks and multiple-choice questions.

The long-writing tasks include writing a news report and a series of paragraphs that express an opinion on a given topic. Organizing your thoughts and planning out your writing ahead of time may help to keep your writing stay focused and organized.

The short-writing tasks are six-lined responses. You are expected to develop one main idea in your written answers, and it is a good idea to use details and important information.

The multiple-choice questions will test your ability to organize information, develop a main idea and use language conventions such as sytax, spelling, grammar and punctuation.

More information on the writing skills required for the OSSLT can be found on the EQAO website at www.eqao.com.

In this resource, you will be walked through two examples of each type of writing activity similar to those you will encounter on the OSSLT. You will find advice from fictional representations of typical Ontario students. Tips will be provided in the form of notes that are "paper-clipped" to your activities for ease of reference.

Tip: Be sure to try the great suggestions in these notes throughout the selections.

You will know you have completed a section when you see the phrase "End of Section" in a grey rectangular box.

End of Section.

News Report: a news story that presents information in a particular format that answers the questions Who? What? Where? When? Why? and How?

. . . .

Hey. What's happening? My name is Liam and I live in Sharbot Lake. Writing news reports is a bit of a process for me because it isn't something I have to do very often in my day-to-day life. What I find challenging is making up all the details. It requires a bit of imagination. Based on the picture and headline, I have to imagine who was involved, what happened—and where, when why and how it happened. Sometimes only some of these questions can be answered. I like to begin by deciding who will be in my news report and create two direct quotes and one indirect quote before even starting to write the actual article. After organizing the story in a logical way, I write the report. News stories are always written in the third person. Unless in a direct quote, I use words such as "she," "he," and "you," instead of words such as "me," "I," "us," or "we." Once I got the hang of it, I actually found writing news reports to be fun and creative.

Writing a News Report

Task:	to write a news report on page 51 pertaining to the headline and picture below. • The news report must relate to the headline **and** the picture provided. • Information and facts to answer the questions Who? What? Where? When? Why? and How? must be made up.
Length:	The space provided indicates the approximate length of the news report.
Purpose and Audience:	to report on an event for newspaper readers

Students Raise Money for Local Charity

Rough Notes
This space below is for rough notes. Nothing you write in this area will be marked.

Tip: Look carefully at the headline AND the photo.

Write your report on the lines provided on page 51.

Hi there. My name is Abigail and I am from Kitchener. I always get organized before writing a news report. After I carefully read the headline and look at the photo, I fill out a Who? What? Where? When? Why? and How? organizer. Fill out the one below to get you started.

Who? (List all the participants who will be in your article. This information comes from the title, the picture and **your imagination.**)

_____

_____

What?

_____

_____

Where?

_____

_____

When?

_____

_____

Why?

_____

_____

How?

_____

_____

Hello. I'm Dhilan and I live in Oshawa. Something that really helped me write a great news report was understanding and using direct and indirect quotes. If you read the newspaper, most articles have them. Direct quotes are the exact words someone says and they are surrounded by quotation marks. Here is an example: "The students were great. They organized the car wash with very little input from the staff," Principal Barker explained. Indirect quotes take the information someone said, but do not share them word-for-word. Here is an example: Educators say that hundreds of students organized a charity car wash completely on their own. Using both types of quotes adds flavour and details to your report.

Using your imagination, create two direct quotes and one indirect quote you can incorporate into your news report based on the headline "Students Raise Money for Local Charity" and the photo on page 48.

_____

_____

_____

_____

Tip: Make sure your direct quotes are inside quotation marks.

_____

_____

_____

_____

Students Raise Money for Local Charity

_____

_____

_____

_____

_____

_____

_____

_____

_____

_____

_____

_____

_____

_____

_____

_____

_____

_____

_____

_____

_____

_____

_____

_____

_____

Tip: Read your report when you are finished writing it to see if it makes sense.

Tip: Organize your report in a logical manner using the information from your graphic organizers.

End of Section.

Writing a News Report

Task:	to write a news report on the next page pertaining to the headline and picture below.
	• The news report must relate to the headline **and** the picture provided.
	• Information and facts to answer the questions Who? What? Where? When? Why? and How? must be made up.
Length:	The space provided indicates the approximate length of the news report.
Purpose and Audience:	to report on an event for newspaper readers

Students Demand Healthy Choices in School Cafeteria

Rough Notes
This space below is for rough notes. Nothing you write in this area will be marked.

Tip: If you don't have enough space here, use scrap paper to organize your thoughts.

Write your report on the lines provided on the next page.

Students Demand Healthy Choices in School Cafeteria

_____

_____

_____

_____

_____

_____

_____

_____

_____

_____

_____

_____

_____

_____

_____

_____

_____

_____

_____

_____

_____

Tip: Double-check to make sure you wrote the report in third person.

End of Section.

Long-Writing Task: expresses an opinion by developing ideas through an introduction, supporting paragraphs and a conclusion.

• •

Hi. I'm Kaitlyn and I am from Thornbury. Expressing my opinion in a series of paragraphs takes some planning for me. First, I decide what my opinion on the assigned topic is, and then I write that down. I then add information about why I hold that opinion and what facts and evidence I base it on. Finally, I put it all together, making sure that it is logical and has at least three paragraphs. I've heard from my teacher that students who write more than the minimum three paragraphs tend to average higher scores on the long-writing questions.

Writing a Series of Paragraphs

Task:	to write at least three paragraphs that express an opinion about the topic listed below
Length:	The space provided indicates the approximate length you are expected to write.
Purpose and Audience:	an interested adult
Topic:	**Should it be mandatory that students stay in school until they are 18 years old?**

Tip: After reading the topic, decide what opinion you will take in your written response.

Write your series of paragraphs on the lines provided on pages 57–58.

Rough Notes
This space below is for rough notes. Nothing you write in this area will be marked.

Should it be mandatory that students stay in school until they are 18 years old?

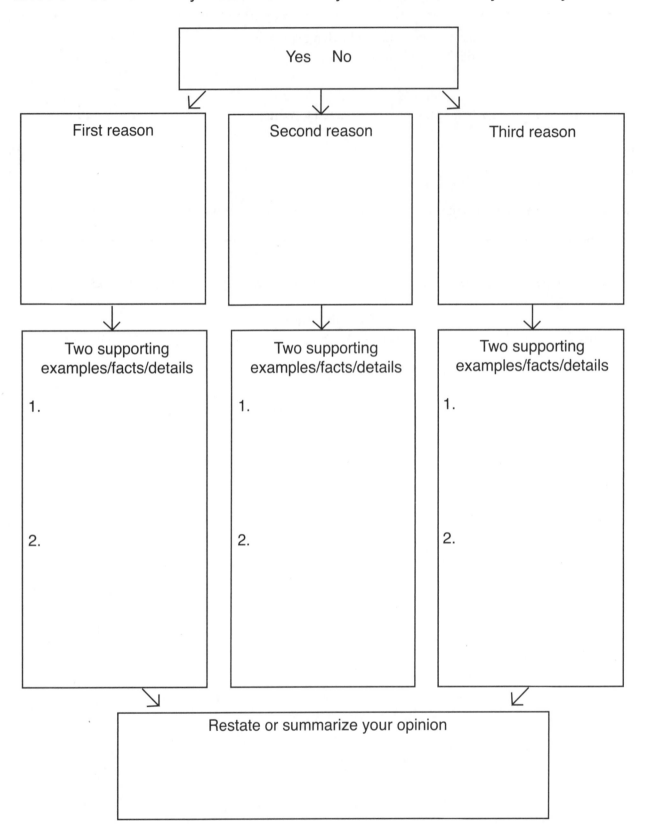

Yes   No

First reason

Second reason

Third reason

Two supporting
examples/facts/details

1.

2.

Two supporting
examples/facts/details

1.

2.

Two supporting
examples/facts/details

1.

2.

Restate or summarize your opinion

Should it be mandatory that students stay in school until they are 18 years old?

Tip: Be clear about your opinion at the beginning and end of your long-writing response.

_____

_____

_____

_____

_____

_____

_____

_____

_____

_____

_____

_____

_____

_____

_____

_____

_____

_____

_____

_____

_____

_____

Continue writing your series of paragraphs on the next page.

Tip: Make sure there are clear divisions between your paragraphs.

End of Section.

Writing a Series of Paragraphs

Task:	to write at least three paragraphs that express an opinion about the topic listed below
Length:	The space provided indicates the approximate length you are expected to write.
Purpose and Audience:	an interested adult
Topic:	**Should the government spend money on space exploration?**

Write your series of paragraphs on the lines provided on the following two pages.

Rough Notes
This space below is for rough notes. Nothing you write in this area will be marked.

Tip: Use this section to make a graphic organizer.

Should the government spend money on space exploration?

Tip: Write three or more paragraphs. Be sure to have a clear introduction, supporting paragraph(s) and conclusion.

Continue writing your series of paragraphs on the next page.

Tip: Back up your opinion with reasons, examples and/or facts.

End of Section.

Short-Writing Task: presents the three writing skills of developing a main idea, organizing information and using conventions

. . . .

I'm Ben and I live in Sioux Lookout. Personally, I actually like short-writing tasks. I think what I like most about them is that I am able to use my own knowledge and experience in the answer instead of having to rely on what other people have said. I develop one main idea, and I like finding specific examples, details and relevant information to support my answer.

Short-Writing Task (Answer in full and complete sentences.)

1 Should teenagers have part-time jobs? Use specific details to explain why or why not.

Tip: Be sure your sentences are written correctly.

_____

_____

_____

_____

_____

_____

Rough Notes

This space below is for rough notes. Nothing you write in this area will be marked.

Tip: It is a good idea to carefully read the question.

End of Section.

Short-Writing Task (Answer in full and complete sentences.)

1 Should every teenager play sports? Use specific details to explain why or why not.

Tip: Reread your response to check for any errors. Correct them if you find any.

_____

_____

_____

_____

_____

_____

Rough Notes
This space below is for rough notes. Nothing you write in this area will be marked.

End of Section.

Multiple-Choice: assesses use of writing conventions such as spelling, grammar, punctuation and syntax

Hello. My name is Davina. I am from London. If I am not careful, the multiple-choice questions can confuse me. I have developed a couple of strategies that really help, though. First, I read and reread the question carefully. Then I read the four answers and rule out any that are incorrect. Sometimes two of them both seem right so I try to choose the *best* or *most* correct answer. I never leave a multiple-choice question blank even if I am not sure of the answer.

Multiple-Choice (Circle the best or most correct answer.)

1 Choose the sentence that is written correctly.

    A Olivia asked, "How are you?"

    B Ethan answered, "I am fine".

    C Emma stated "It is cold outside."

    D Lucas queried, 'what day is the dance?'

Tip: Look at the punctuation carefully in question #1.

2 How is the following paragraph organized?

There are many differences between apples and oranges. Although they are both fruit, oranges have a much thicker skin and need to be peeled in order to eat easily. On the other hand, apples can be eaten skin and all. They are both popular fruit and many people enjoy these healthy and tasty foods.

    A by order of importance

    B by cause and effect

    C by chronological order

    D by comparison and contrast

3 Choose the sentence that is written correctly.

    A Jade is going too the park.

    B Logan wants to go to.

    C Madison loves pandas too.

    D Owen wants too see his friend.

4 Choose the sentence that is written correctly

    A Maya attended central Secondary school.

    B Mr. Maltby taught a Class in Phys. Ed.

    C East Secondary School had a great Selection of Computer classes.

    D Jackson went to school in Orangeville.

Multiple-Choice (Circle the best or most correct answer.)

1 Choose the sentence that is written correctly.

    A Me and Riley are going to the mall.

    B My mom gave snacks to Ava and I.

    C Ryan and me went swimming.

    D Hannah and I went to a concert.

2 Which sentence does not belong in the paragraph?

(1) Volunteering benefits young people. (2) It gives them skills and teaches them responsibility. (3) Volunteering helps them gain valuable experience for future decisions. (4) Many retired people volunteer. (5) Volunteering is a great way to prepare for the future.

    A Sentence 2

    B Sentence 3

    C Sentence 4

    D Sentence 5

3 Choose the sentence that is written correctly.

    A Nicholas is turning 16 next week.

    B Peyton want to know how old you are.

    C Isabella and Jacob is hungry.

    D Matt were going to see him.

4 Choose the sentence that is written correctly

    A The vacation photo's were on the computer.

    B Our houses door was broken.

    C We went out to eat at Jenns restaurant.

    D The boat's motor was broken.

Tip: If you don't know the answer at all, make an educated guess.

End of Section.

SECTION 3

Section 3: The OSSLT Testing Lab

The OSSLT Literacy Testing Lab consists of two booklets. You will have 75 minutes to complete each booklet, with a 15 minute break between them. You will also be allotted 10 minutes to complete a questionnaire at the end of the test.

The OSSLT has operational items and field-test items. Operational items will be scored, whereas field-test items are used to test new questions. Don't worry; the non-scored questions are less than 20% of the testing time.

Make sure that your answers are filled in on the Student Answer Sheet. Your written responses can be written directly on the *Test Booklet*. For multiple-choice questions, you will either get a score of "1" for the correct answer or a score of "0" for an incorrect or blank answer.

This is one more reason to guess instead of leaving a question blank if you don't know the answer!

Both short- and long-writing answers have two scoring rubrics: one for developing your topic and another for proper use of conventions.

You must reach a score of approximately 70% in order to pass the test.

More information on how the OSSLT is scored can be found on the EQAO website at www.eqao.com.

OSSLT Test: timed assessment of reading and writing skills

Hey. My name is Alex and I am from Peterborough. I took the OSSLT last year and the biggest hurdle for me was that it was timed. I knew it was going to be timed, but I never practised dividing my time up before. I did a lot of practice developing my skills for the test, but I didn't work on time-management skills. I found that I was so focused on doing everything right and checking and double-checking my work that I ran out of time before I had finished the first booklet. So, when it came time to work on the second booklet, I looked at all the tasks in it first and made sure to divide my time between all of them. I actually finished five minutes early and then went back over the test booklet to do a thorough check and proofread.

Hey there. I'm Zach and I'm from Woodstock. Before there was online testing options, I had to get used to the answer sheet. In all my practice, I just circled the answers right on the practice sheet. However, in the test all the multiple-choice answers had to be marked in circles on an answer sheet. The multiple-choice questions are marked using a computer, so it is important to mark your answer in the correct line on your answer sheet. It doesn't hurt to double-check before filling in the circle to make sure you are marking the right one. Cut out the Student Answer Sheet on the next page so you can use it to practise when you complete the practice test.

The OSSLT Literacy Lab

Student Answer Sheet

Practice Test Booklets

BOOKLET 1

Section A

1. (A) (B) (C) (D)
2. (A) (B) (C) (D)
3. (A) (B) (C) (D)
4. (A) (B) (C) (D)
5. (A) (B) (C) (D)
6. Respond in booklet.

Section B

1. (A) (B) (C) (D)
2. (A) (B) (C) (D)
3. (A) (B) (C) (D)
4. (A) (B) (C) (D)
5. (A) (B) (C) (D)

Section C

1. (A) (B) (C) (D)
2. (A) (B) (C) (D)
3. (A) (B) (C) (D)
4. (A) (B) (C) (D)
5. (A) (B) (C) (D)
6. (A) (B) (C) (D)
7. Respond in booklet.

Name: _____

Section D

1. Respond in booklet.

Section E

1. Respond in booklet.

Section F

1. (A) (B) (C) (D)
2. (A) (B) (C) (D)
3. (A) (B) (C) (D)
4. (A) (B) (C) (D)
5. (A) (B) (C) (D)
6. (A) (B) (C) (D)
7. Respond in booklet.

End of Booklet 1

BOOKLET 2

Section G

1. Respond in booklet.

Section H

1. (A) (B) (C) (D)
2. (A) (B) (C) (D)
3. (A) (B) (C) (D)
4. (A) (B) (C) (D)

Section I

1. (A) (B) (C) (D)
2. (A) (B) (C) (D)
3. (A) (B) (C) (D)
4. (A) (B) (C) (D)
5. (A) (B) (C) (D)
6. (A) (B) (C) (D)
7. (A) (B) (C) (D)
8. (A) (B) (C) (D)
9. (A) (B) (C) (D)

Section J

1. (A) (B) (C) (D)
2. (A) (B) (C) (D)
3. (A) (B) (C) (D)
4. (A) (B) (C) (D)
5. (A) (B) (C) (D)
6. Respond in booklet.
7. Respond in booklet.

Section K

1. Respond in booklet.

Section L

1. (A) (B) (C) (D)
2. (A) (B) (C) (D)
3. (A) (B) (C) (D)
4. (A) (B) (C) (D)
5. (A) (B) (C) (D)
6. (A) (B) (C) (D)

Questionnaire

Section M

1. (Y) (N)
2. (Y) (N)
3. (Y) (N)
4. (Y) (N)
5. (Y) (N)
6. (Y) (N)
7. (Y) (N)
8. (Y) (N)
9. (Y) (N)

End of Test

	BOOKLET
Practice Test Booklet	**1**

The OSSLT Literacy Lab

Practice Literacy Test
BOOKLET 1

Instructions for the Practice Literacy Test:

- You will have 75 minutes to complete this booklet.

- Read all passages and instructions carefully.

- Use only a pencil or a pen with either blue or black ink.

- Mark multiple-choice answers directly on the Student Answer Sheet. Make sure to fill in the corresponding circle completely.

- Write all your open-resonse, short- and long-writing answers directly in the *Practice Test Booklet*.

Instructions for the OSSLT can be found on the EQAO website at www.eqao.com.

Read the selection below and answer the following questions.

High School Students Struggle to Get Volunteer Hours

1. Hundreds of Ontario Grade 12 students scramble to graduate at the last minute because they have not done their 40 mandatory hours of volunteer work, educators say.

2. To help tackle the issue, Ontario has begun to let Grade 8 grads count volunteer work they do in the summer before Grade 9. The province also now requires all students from Grade 7 to 12 to use an on-line tool to plan courses, get career ideas—and plan where they'll do volunteer hours.

3. "Some don't know what to do, and scramble over the summer to get their hours by Aug. 31 so they can graduate," said John McPhee, Toronto District School Board's program coordinator of guidance, career and adolescent development.

4. Toronto television producer Christiane MacKenzie tried helping her younger brother find somewhere to do his 40 hours when he was in high school and was shocked at how daunting it can be for kids.

5. She has spent the past three years developing a breezy, student-friendly, non-profit website to help steer teens to dozens of legitimate charities that take volunteers under 18—complete with the name of who to call—and lets students track their hours digitally.

6. "Not everyone has volunteer opportunities at their fingertips," said MacKenzie, "so we need to move charities and education into the digital age."

7. John McPhee welcomes the site, partly because "it's hip—with celebrity interviews, it's almost like a music video about volunteering."

8. Mackenzie also is planning a weekly TV show where a student will visit a charity and surprise-celebrities will promote volunteering.

9. Toronto Grade 11 student Leah Giles took part in one of the upcoming TV shows, where she visited a local charity. While the 16-year-old has done 22 hours with her local humane society, she will use MacKenzie's website in January to plan where to do the rest.

10. "A lot of the time, what kids do is just work for their uncle's store or something, but these big organizations are really interesting," said Leah. "You can be part of an organization that actually changes something."

Adapted from the article "Ontario high school students struggle to get their volunteer hours" by Louise Brown, published in *Toronto Star*, December 20, 2013. Licensed from *Toronto Star* for republication in *The OSSLT Literacy Lab*—Torstar Syndication Services.

Multiple-Choice (Mark the best answer on the Student Answer Sheet.)

1 Why did television producer Christiane Mackenzie start a non-profit website?

   A to help all students track their volunteer hours digitally.

   B to help students with the daunting task of finding places to get their volunteer hours

   C to help her younger brother find somewhere to do his 40 hours of volunteer service

   D to hire students to run the website

2 Why has Ontario begun to let Grade 8 grads count volunteer work they do in the summer before Grade 9 toward their required 40 hours?

   A because summer is the best time to volunteer

   B because charities need more volunteers

   C because students are scrambling to complete their volunteer hours before graduation

   D because younger students enjoy volunteering more than older students

3 How is this news report organized?

   A by comparison and contrast

   B as steps in a sequence

   C as cause and effect

   D as problem and solution

4 Why are the words "student-friendly" hyphenated in paragraph 5?

   A to indicate a compound adjective

   B to indicate they are two words

   C to indicate they are split to the next line

   D to make them easier to read

5 Why does Leah think volunteering is important?

   A The hours are needed to graduate.

   B It is rewarding to make a difference.

   C It is fun.

   D It is a great way to get experience for a job.

Turn the page to complete Section A.

6 Are volunteer hours a useful part of the high school experience? Use a specific detail from the selection to support your answer.

_____

_____

_____

_____

_____

_____

Rough Notes

This space below is for rough notes. Nothing you write in this area will be marked.

End of Section A.

Continue to Section B.

Multiple-Choice (Mark the best answer on the Student Answer Sheet.)

1 Which of the following is a complete sentence?

    A Walking quietly under the bridge.

    B Because Austin ran a marathon.

    C Sara caught the ball.

    D The lovely sunny and warm day.

2 Choose the sentence that is written correctly.

    A The gardener's weeded the rock garden.

    B We went over to Lily's house.

    C The cars door was broken.

    D The bicycles tire was flat.

3 Choose the best option that combines the information in the boldfaced statements:

Tablets are convenient.
Computers have bigger screens.
Many people prefer to read email on their cell phones.
Cell phones are very portable.

    A Although tablets are convenient and computers have bigger screens, many people prefer reading email on their cell phones because they are very portable.

    B Tablets are convenient, computers have bigger screens, many people prefer to read email on their cell phones; they are very portable.

    C Tablets are convenient and computers have biggers screens but many people prefer to read email on their cell phones and they are very portable.

    D Tablets are convenient, computers have bigger screens because many people prefer to read email on their cell phones or they are very portable.

4 Choose the best word to fill in the blank.

The currency is dollars in North America, _____ it is pounds in the United Kingdom.

    A because

    B whereas

    C if

    D so

5 What punctuation is missing from this sentence?

If I wear my running shoes on a snowy day I might fall on the sidewalk.

    A a colon

    B a period

    C a semicolon

    D a comma

End of Section B.

Continue to Section C.

Read the selection below and answer the following questions.

There is a movement spreading across North America to return to houses that are less than 93 square metres. This tiny house trend was made popular in recent years by Jay Shafer and Gregory Johnson who founded the Small House Society in 2002. Shafer designed a tiny house for Johnson, and then Shafer continued on to offer plans for tiny houses on wheels through a company called Tumblewood Tiny House Company and then Four Light Houses. After Hurricane Katrina in 2005, Marianne Cusato developed Katrina Cottages that started at 28.6 square metres. They were created to provide a solution for a disaster zone, but gained a wider interest from the general public and resort developers. The financial crises of 2007–2010 also fuelled this movement as small homes were more affordable to acquire and maintain. Many tiny homes are more ecologically friendly too. Recently, small homes have been getting increased media coverage in the news and on television shows. Still, only about 1% of home buyers acquire what would be considered a small home. Although this is a tiny percentage, the trend is growing.

5

10

Multiple-Choice (Mark the best answer on the Student Answer Sheet.)

1 How is this selection organized?

    A past to present

    B specific to general

    C least important to most important

    D most important to least important

2 What supports the idea that more and more people are interested in the small home trend?

    A The homes solve a problem.

    B The homes are more affordable.

    C The homes are getting increased media coverage.

    D The homes are more ecological.

3 Why were Katrina Cottages first developed?

    A to offer a solution to the financial crises of 2007–2010

    B to satisfy resort developers who were interested in the concept

    C to provide a solution when homes were destroyed in a disaster

    D to improve ecological friendliness

4 What word is closest in meaning to "fuelled" as used in line 9?

    A shaped

    B prepared

    C reassured

    D encouraged

5 What is **not** a reason the tiny house trend is spreading across North America?

    A Catastrophes have destroyed many people's homes.

    B They are pleasing to look at.

    C They are economical to purchase.

    D They are good for the environment.

6 What is most likely the reason that about 99% of home buyers do not acquire a small home?

    A They have not been victim of a disaster.

    B They wish to have more room.

    C They do not care about the environment.

    D They were not affected by a financial crisis.

Turn the page to complete Section C.

7 State a main idea of this selection, and provide one specific detail from the selection that supports it.

_____

_____

_____

_____

_____

Rough Notes
This space below is for rough notes. Nothing you write in this area will be marked.

End of Section C.

Continue to Section D.

Short-Writing Task (Answer in full and complete sentences.)

1 What is your favourite season of the year? Use specific details to explain why.

_____

_____

_____

_____

_____

Rough Notes
This space below is for rough notes. Nothing you write in this area will be marked.

End of Section D.

Continue to Section E.

Writing a News Report

Task:	to write a news report on the next page pertaining to the headline and picture below.
	• The news report must relate to the headline **and** the picture provided.
	• Information and facts to answer the questions Who? What? Where? When? Why? and How? must be made up.
Length:	The space provided indicates the approximate length of the news report.
Purpose and Audience:	to report on an event for newspaper readers

Students Save Local Dog Park

Rough Notes
This space below is for rough notes. Nothing you write in this area will be marked.

Students Save Local Dog Park

End of Section E.

Continue to Section F.

Read the selection below and answer the following questions.

A carbon footprint is the total amount of greenhouse gas emissions caused by an organization, an event, a product or a person. Carbon emissions that are released into the atmosphere are thought to contribute to climate change. Although carbon emissions are an environmental problem, there are many simple things people can do to help reduce their personal carbon footprint and help the planet. For example, 5 reusing and recycling are easy ways to prevent new products being made unnecessarily. Wearing vintage clothing and remembering to recycle plastics, cans and paper are not only simple things to do, but are also in fashion and considered to be vogue. Choosing energy-efficient lighting and unplugging gadgets when not in use cut down electricity consumption. If it is available, consider taking public transportation or keep vehicles 10 tuned up. This helps to reduce fuel usage. Planting trees, being careful with water usage and composting are also top-notch ways to lower your negative impact on the environment. The earth is a spectacular place and a home we share with each other. Making an effort to lower our carbon footprint is not only easy, but a good way to respect the planet.

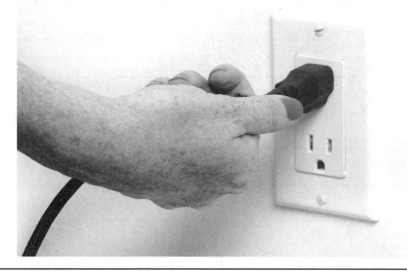

Multiple-Choice (Mark the best answer on the Student Answer Sheet.)

1 What does the word "it" refer to in line 10?

    A public transportation

    B climate change

    C carbon footprint

    D recycling

2 What word is closest in meaning to "vogue" as used in line 8?

    A thoughtful

    B trendy

    C helpful

    D correct

3 How is the selection organized?

    A in chronological order

    B through a comparison

    C as a description

    D as a problem and solution

4 According to this selection, what does "carbon footprint" mean?

    A greenhouse gas released into the atmosphere

    B climate change

    C reusing and recycling

    D unplugging your gadgets

5 Why is the statement in lines 13–14 an effective conclusion to this selection?

    A It connects conserving energy with organizations.

    B It suggests that environmental issues are not relevant.

    C It suggests that small and easy personal changes can help reduce our carbon footprint.

    D It suggests that lowering our carbon footprint is impossible.

6 What is the main purpose for the comma in line 10?

    A to introduce a comparison

    B to introduce a clarification

    C to separate two main ideas

    D to indicate a series in a list

Turn the page to complete Section F.

7 State a main idea of this selection, and provide one specific detail from the selection that supports it.

_____

_____

_____

_____

_____

Rough Notes

This space below is for rough notes. Nothing you write in this area will be marked.

End of Booklet 1.

	BOOKLET
Practice Test Booklet	**2**

The OSSLT Literacy Lab

Practice Literacy Test

BOOKLET 2

Instructions for the Practice Literacy Test:

- You will have 75 minutes to complete this booklet.

- Read all passages and instructions carefully.

- Use only a pencil or a pen with either blue or black ink.

- Mark multiple-choice answers directly on the Student Answer Sheet. Make sure to fill in the corresponding circle completely.

- Write all your open-resonse, short- and long-writing answers directly in the *Practice Test Booklet*.

Instructions for the OSSLT can be found on the EQAO website at www.eqao.com.

Writing a Series of Paragraphs

Task:	to write at least three paragraphs that express an opinion about the topic listed below
Length:	The space provided indicates the approximate length you are expected to write.
Purpose and Audience:	an interested adult
Topic:	**Is the use of technology making teenagers less social?**

Write your series of paragraphs on the lines provided on the following two pages.

Rough Notes
This space below is for rough notes. Nothing you write in this area will be marked.

Is the use of technology making teenagers less social?

_____

_____

_____

_____

_____

_____

_____

_____

_____

_____

_____

_____

_____

_____

_____

_____

_____

_____

Continue writing your series of paragraphs on the next page.

End of Section G.

Continue to Section H.

Multiple-Choice (Mark the best answer on the Student Answer Sheet.)

1 Choose the sentence that is written correctly.

    A When he finished drawing Dan went to the store.

    B When he finished drawing, Dan went to the store.

    C When he finished drawing Dan, went to the store.

    D When he finished, drawing Dan went to the store.

2 Choose the correct option to fill in the blank.

Emma _____ the results of her test tomorrow.

    A got

    B get

    C has get

    D will get

3 Choose the correct option to fill in the blank.

Hannah couldn't go to the concert _____ the tickets were too expensive.

    A however

    B although

    C because

    D so that

4 Which of the following is a complete sentence?

    A Kayla threw the papers away.

    B Because Caleb ran quickly.

    C Calling to his friends.

    D The cold and shivery day.

End of Section H.

Continue to Section I.

Read the selection below and answer the following questions.

Hadfield Is Out of This World

Photo Credit: NASA

Astronaut Colonel Chris Hadfield is known for a lot of firsts: the first Canadian space shuttle mission specialist; the first Canadian to operate the Canadarm in orbit; the first and only Canadian to ever board the Russian space station, *Mir*; the first Canadian to leave a spacecraft and float freely in space, but becoming the first Canadian commander of the *International Space Station* (or ISS) on March 13, 2013, might be the most memorable of all. 1

Chris was born in Sarnia, Ontario and raised in Milton. When Chris was only nine years old, he watched Neil Armstrong walk on the moon. He attributes this as the spark that ignited his interest in space travel. 2

With an educational background in mechanical engineering, Chris became a fighter pilot and then a test pilot. He was chosen to become one of four new Canadian astronauts from a pool of 5,330 applicants in 1992. 3

Although Chris was in space in 1995 and 2001, his final mission was Expedition 34/35 to the ISS, and it began when he was launched aboard the Russian spacecraft, *Soyuz*, on December 19, 2012. 4

On March 13, 2013, Hadfield became commander of the space station. He was described by *Forbes Magazine* as "perhaps the most social media savvy astronaut to leave earth." With the help of his son, Evan, he obtained over one million Twitter followers. 5

Besides performing his usual duties on board the *International Space Station* such as conducting experiments, exercising and commanding the station, Chris took thousands of breathtaking photos, created videos explaining how things are done differently in space, answered questions from the media and students via video link, and recorded music.

6

Hadfield sang "Is Somebody Singing" in space, a song created in collaboration with the band The Barenaked Ladies. He sang with singers across Canada for the national "Music Monday" program. Hadfield also released a music video recorded on the *International Space Station* of a modified version of the song "Space Oddity" by David Bowie. The video received over 22 million views on YouTube.

7

Many believe that Colonel Hadfield's popularity and excellent use of social media has brought heightened attention to space exploration. He took fantastic pictures, made space accessible, and "brought us along with him." Chris Hadfield is certainly one Canadian who is out of this world.

8

Photo Credit: NASA

Written for *The OSSLT Literacy Lab* by Heather Down, author of *Postcards from Space: The Chris Hadfield Story* published by Wintertickle Press, 2013. Used with permission.

Multiple-Choice (Mark the best answer on the Student Answer Sheet.)

1 When did Chris first become interested in space travel?

    A when he became a fighter pilot

    B when he studied mechanical engineering

    C when he watched Neil Armstrong walk on the moon

    D when he became a test pilot

2 Which word is closest in meaning to "savvy" as used in paragraph 5?

    A wise

    B stylish

    C talented

    D capable

3 Why is a colon used in paragraph 1?

    A It joins two independent clauses.

    B It introduces a list.

    C It emphasizes content to follow.

    D It joins elements of a series.

4 How did Chris travel to the ISS for Expedition 34/35?

    A He went in the space shuttle.

    B He went to the space station *Mir*.

    C He went in the *Soyuz*.

    D He went in an *Apollo* rocket.

5 What statistic indicated that Chris's activities on the ISS were popular?

    A There were 5,330 applicants in 1992.

    B He had over one million Twitter followers.

    C He was in space in 1995, 2001, and 2012–2013.

    D The ISS Expedition numbers were 34/35.

6 What was one activity that Chris did **not** perform on the ISS?

    A record videos

    B speak with media and students

    C sing songs with musicians

    D create paintings about space

7 What literacy device is used in paragraph 8?

    A metaphor

    B simile

    C pun

    D personification

8 Why did Chris Hadfield's expedition bring heightened attention to space exploration?

    A his popularity and use of social media

    B his unique skills as a pilot

    C his ability to conduct experiments in space

    D his Canadian background

Multiple-Choice (Mark the best answer on the Student Answer Sheet.)

9 What is the purpose of the quotation marks around "Is Somebody Singing" in paragraph 7?

    A to set it apart

    B to indicate it is a direct quote

    C to indicate it is a TV show

    D to indicate it is the name of a song

End of Section I.

Continue to Section J.

Read the selection below and answer the following questions.

Danica laced up her skates carefully. She was feeling the pressure of being the goalie today more than ever. Today their team was playing for the regional championship. As she pulled on her gear, she felt her heart skip a beat. 1

"How are you feeling?" Coach asked. 2

"Not too bad," Danica lied. She felt terrified. 3

"That's my best goalie," Coach smiled. 4

Danica gulped and tried to return the smile, but it was hopeless. She couldn't fake confidence. 5

Coach was just about to walk away, but she noticed Danica's expression. 6

"You know, Danica. Don't take all the pressure on. You are the goalie, I know. But it takes a team to win or lose, not just one person." 7

"Yes, I know, Coach, but it doesn't always feel that way. I feel like I am letting everybody down if a goal goes through." 8

"That is an understandable way to feel, Danica. But really, you need to balance your anxiety with having fun too. A few nerves are good to keep you sharp and playing your best. However, too much worry can have the opposite effect on your performance." 9

"I know. But, sometimes I just don't know how to handle the pressure. I don't know what to do." 10

"Well, here are a couple of things I used to do when I played. Firstly, and most importantly, remember that it is just a game. Yes, it is important to do your best, but at the end of the day, it is a game. Secondly, remember you've practised and played all season, so you are prepared for today. You deserve to be here and you earned it. And, finally, take a few minutes before going on to sit back, breathe deeply and visualize everything going well." 11

"Those are good tips, Coach. Thank you. I think I am going to start with your advice right now." 12

Multiple-Choice (Mark the best answer on the Student Answer Sheet.)

1 Why couldn't Danica return Coach's smile?

   A She was sad.

   B She couldn't fake confidence.

   C She didn't like her coach.

   D She didn't like being a goalie.

2 Which word is closest in meaning to "performance" as used in paragraph 9?

   A concert

   B fuss

   C actions

   D skating

3 How does Coach know Danica is nervous about the game?

   A Danica tells her.

   B It is an important game.

   C Danica avoids the coach.

   D Danica looks nervous.

4 Why does Danica feel so much pressure for this particular game?

   A She feels that she lets her team down if a goal goes in the net.

   B She is playing for the regional championship.

   C She is the first-string goalie.

   D She has worked hard to be on the team.

5 According to the selection, why should Danica not worry so much about the championship?

   A She is doing her best.

   B It is just a game.

   C She can visualize success.

   D She is prepared for the day.

Turn the page to complete Section J.

6 Identify the techniques that Coach uses to help Danica calm her nerves. Use specific details from the selection to support your answer.

_____

_____

_____

_____

_____

_____

7 Identify an example of how Danica feels pressure being the team's goalie. Use specific details from the selection to support your answer.

_____

_____

_____

_____

_____

_____

Rough Notes
This space below is for rough notes. Nothing you write in this area will be marked.

End of Section J.

Continue to Section K.

Short-Writing Task (Answer in full and complete sentences.)

1 What is the best advice you could give to someone going into Grade 9? Use specific details to explain your answer.

_____

_____

_____

_____

_____

_____

Rough Notes

This space below is for rough notes. Nothing you write in this area will be marked.

End of Section K.

Continue to Section L.

Read the selection below and answer the following questions.

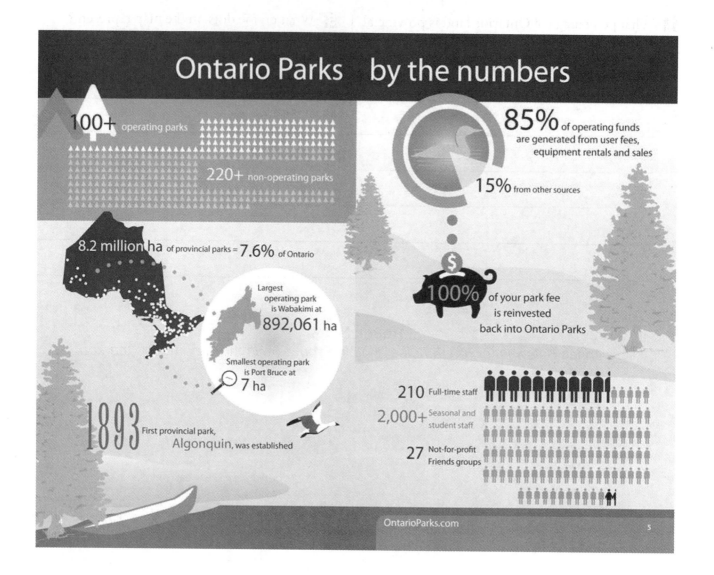

Credit: Ontario Ministry of Natural Resources, Ontario Parks "Ontario Parks by the Numbers," *Parks Guide 2014*, pages 4-5. Used with permission.

Multiple-Choice (Mark the best answer on the Student Answer Sheet.)

1 What percentage of Ontario's land is provincial parkland?

    A 85%

    B 15%

    C 100%

    D 7.6%

2 What symbol in this graphic text provides a visual for comparing operating parks to non-operating parks?

    A ducks

    B trees

    C people

    D dots

3 What was the first provincial park?

    A Algonquin

    B Port Bruce

    C Wabakimi

    D Awenda

4 How is the graphical representation of the staff organized?

    A by comparison and contrast

    B by chronological order

    C by problem and solution

    D by description

5 What do the dots on the map represent?

    A number of staff

    B money distribution

    C number of parks

    D location of parks

6 What word is closest in meaning to "generated" (by 85%) as used in the selection?

    A energized

    B created

    C taken

    D lost

End of Section L.

Continue to Section M.

Background Information (Mark your answers on the Student Answer Sheet.)

The OSSLT will ask you questions about your background in order to see how students with different experiences do on the test. More information on the Student Questionnaire can be found on the EQAO website at www.eqao.com

This survey is not scored. There is no right or wrong answer. Read each question carefully. If no answer seems exactly right, fill in the circle on the Student Answer Sheet with the response closest to what you want to say. Here are some practice background questions to think about.

1 Is English your first language?

   Y Yes   **N** No

2 Do you read non-fiction books?

   Y Yes   **N** No

3 Do you read newspapers?

   Y Yes   **N** No

4 Do you read magazines?

   Y Yes   **N** No

5 Do you read emails?

   Y Yes   **N** No

6 Do you have books at home?

   Y Yes   **N** No

7 Do you have newspapers at home?

   Y Yes   **N** No

8 Do you write letters or emails?

   Y Yes   **N** No

9 Do you write stories?

   Y Yes   **N** No

End of test.

Afterword: concluding remarks in a book, either by the author or someone else

Hi. My name is Cole and I am from Belleville. I am graduating this year, but there was a time when I wasn't sure that I would. When I was in Grade 10, I was worried I wouldn't pass the OSSLT. I was concerned what my friends might think of me if I failed so I *purposely* didn't prepare. That way, when I failed I could say, "I didn't try." And, of course, that is exactly what happened. When I got the results, my mom sat me down and asked what was going on. When I confessed what I had done, she explained to me that I had nothing to lose if I actually tried my best. So, I opted to take the test again in Grade 11. This time, I prepared. I worked through several sample tests, had a workbook and read a variety of materials such as magazines and online news reports. I practised my writing skills and actually paid attention to proofreading my work. I was much more prepared and, more importantly, I actually tried to do well on the test. And, what do you know? I passed. My mom was always spouting this famous quote, "Better to have tried and failed than to have never tried at all." Now I understand what she meant.

Hello. I'm Jordyn and I am from Mississauga. I worked really hard to prepare for the OSSLT. I read as much as I could. I took an after-school remedial course and I worked through several workbooks dealing with literacy. My dad worked with me on weekends going over my reading and writing skills. I made sure to get a good night's sleep the night before the test and to eat a good breakfast. I thought I was ready. I was focused and did my best. You can imagine how I felt when I got my results and found out I didn't pass. I was really upset. My parents and I went in to discuss my situation with my guidance counsellor, Mr. Syed. He was understanding and told me that I didn't need to be so hard on myself. He felt that maybe it would be a good idea to request to take the Ontario Secondary School Literacy Course (OSSLC) instead of writing the test again. I can take it in Grade 12 and still graduate. Wow! What a relief.

Final questions to think about:

- Do you feel prepared for the OSSLT? Why or why not?
- When it comes to literacy, what are your strengths? What are your weaknesses?
- What additional things can you do to prepare for the test?
- What things do you need to remember on the day of the test?
- What is your plan of action when you receive your results?
- What are you most nervous about?
- What are you most confident about?

Thoughts

_____

_____

_____

_____

_____

_____

_____

_____

_____

Notes